Business 360°: Unlocking Computer Application

NotesKaro

Published by NotesKaro Inc, 2025.

BUSINESS 360°: UNLOCKING COMPUTER APPLICATION

First edition. May 23, 2025.

ISBN: 979-8231637508

Written by NotesKaro.

Table of Contents

Chapter 1: Advanced Excel Functions and Business Modeling

IN TODAY'S DATA-DRIVEN world, Microsoft Excel has evolved from being just a spreadsheet tool to a powerful platform for business analytics, financial modeling, and decision-making. This chapter dives deep into the most essential advanced features of Excel that are widely used in the business world, including lookup functions, pivot tables, dashboards, data validation, goal seek, and scenario manager.

1. Lookup Functions

VLOOKUP (Vertical Lookup)

VLOOKUP IS USED TO search a value in the first column of a table and return a value in the same row from another column.

Syntax:

VLOOKUP(lookup_value, table_array, col_index_num, [range_lookup])

Example: Suppose you have a product ID and you want to find the product name from a table:

Product ID	Product Name
101	Pen
102	Pencil

=VLOOKUP(102, A2:B3, 2, FALSE)

Result: "Pencil"

HLOOKUP (Horizontal Lookup)

HLOOKUP IS SIMILAR to VLOOKUP but it searches in the first row and returns data from a specific row below.

Example: Suppose you have data arranged in rows:

	A	B
ID	101	102
Name	Pen	Pencil

=HLOOKUP(102, A1:B2, 2, FALSE)

Result: "Pencil"

XLOOKUP (Modern Lookup)

XLOOKUP IS THE NEWER and more flexible function introduced in Excel 365.

Syntax:

XLOOKUP(lookup_value, lookup_array, return_array, [if_not_found])

Example:

=XLOOKUP(102, A2:A3, B2:B3, "Not Found")

2. Pivot Tables

PIVOT TABLES SUMMARIZE large datasets and help analyze data trends and patterns. They allow users to rearrange (or pivot) rows and columns to see different summaries.

Steps to Create a Pivot Table:

1. Select your data.
2. Go to "Insert" > "Pivot Table"
3. Drag fields into Rows, Columns, Values, and Filters.

Example Use Case: If you have sales data for multiple regions and months, a pivot table can summarize total sales per region or per product.

Benefits:

- Quick summarization
- Easy comparison
- Drill-down capability

3. Dashboards

DASHBOARDS IN EXCEL are visual representations of data, combining charts, tables, and KPIs in one view.

Key Elements:

- Pivot Tables
- Charts (Bar, Line, Pie)
- Slicers
- Conditional Formatting

Example: An executive dashboard might show total monthly revenue, profit margins, and top-performing regions using dynamic charts and slicers for real-time updates.

Why Dashboards Matter in Business:

- Real-time insights
- Better decision-making
- Professional reporting

4. Data Validation

DATA VALIDATION ENSURES that users enter valid data into cells.

Steps to Use:

1. Select cells
2. Go to "Data" > "Data Validation"
3. Set criteria (e.g., list of options, number range)

Examples:

- Create a dropdown for departments: HR, Sales, IT
- Restrict entry between 1 and 100

Business Relevance:

- Reduces data entry errors
- Ensures consistent data collection

5. Goal Seek

GOAL SEEK IS A REVERSE calculation tool used to find the input value that will achieve a desired result.

Steps:

1. Go to "Data" > "What-If Analysis" > "Goal Seek"
2. Set the target value for a cell

3. Specify the cell to change

Example: Find what price per unit is needed to reach a revenue of $10,000.

Business Use:

- Break-even analysis
- Target achievement

6. Scenario Manager

SCENARIO MANAGER ALLOWS users to create and compare multiple business scenarios.

Steps:

1. Go to "Data" > "What-If Analysis" > "Scenario Manager"
2. Add scenarios with different input values
3. Generate a summary report

Example: Create scenarios for "Best Case", "Worst Case", and "Expected Case" with varying costs and revenues.

Benefits in Business:

- Decision-making support
- Risk analysis
- Financial forecasting

Conclusion

ADVANCED EXCEL FEATURES like lookup functions, pivot tables, dashboards, and scenario tools are indispensable in today's business environment. They not only enhance productivity but also empower professionals to make smarter, data-driven decisions. This chapter has introduced these tools in a human-friendly manner with real examples so you can apply them immediately in your academic or professional life.

Mastering these tools doesn't require being an expert in programming; just a consistent practice with real-world data can transform your efficiency. In the next chapter, we will delve deeper into Microsoft Word and its business applications, covering formal document creation, professional formatting, and much more.

Chapter 2: Microsoft Word for Business Documentation

IN THE MODERN BUSINESS environment, effective communication and professional documentation are key drivers of success. Among the most widely used tools for business documentation is Microsoft Word. With its rich feature set and user-friendly interface, Word allows professionals to create, format, and share documents that are not only informative but also visually appealing. This chapter explores how to leverage Microsoft Word for various business documentation tasks including creating reports, writing business letters, using templates, mail merge, and applying professional formatting techniques.

1. Importance of Microsoft Word in Business

MICROSOFT WORD IS MORE than just a word processor. It is a powerful tool for creating polished business documents such as reports, proposals, contracts, brochures, and emails. Its flexibility and wide range of features allow users to tailor documents for different purposes and audiences.

Some reasons for its wide use include:

- **Ease of use**: Intuitive interface and drag-and-drop features.
- **Collaboration**: Integration with OneDrive and SharePoint allows multiple users to edit simultaneously.
- **Templates**: Pre-designed formats save time and ensure consistency.

- **Formatting tools**: Comprehensive tools for fonts, headings, colors, spacing, and alignment.

---

2. Creating Business Reports

BUSINESS REPORTS SUMMARIZE data, research, or performance for decision-making. Here's how to create a simple business report:

Step-by-step Example:

1. Open Word and select Blank Document.
2. Add a Title: "Quarterly Sales Report – Q2 2025." Use Heading 1.
3. Add a Table of Contents (References > Table of Contents).
4. Insert section headers: Introduction, Data Summary, Analysis, Conclusion.
5. Insert charts using Insert > Chart (e.g., pie chart for market share).
6. Use Page Layout > Margins > Narrow for more space.

Tips:

- Use bullet points to list key findings.
- Highlight important figures in bold or different color.
- Use headers and subheaders for readability.

---

3. Business Letters

BUSINESS LETTERS ARE formal communications between organizations or with clients. They should follow a specific structure:

Structure of a Business Letter:

- Sender's address
- Date
- Receiver's address
- Salutation (e.g., Dear Mr. Sharma,)
- Body: Introduction, Main Content, Conclusion
- Closing (e.g., Sincerely, Regards)
- Signature

Example Letter:

Inkwhirl Publishing

Sector 12, Delhi NCR

May 23, 2025

Mr. Ajay Singh

Procurement Head

EduTech Pvt. Ltd.

Subject: Proposal Submission

Dear Mr. Singh,

We are pleased to submit our proposal for your upcoming digital education project...

Sincerely,

Mrigendra Bharti

Founder & CEO

4. Using Templates

TEMPLATES SAVE TIME and ensure that your documents follow a consistent format.

Steps to use templates in Word:

1. Go to File > New.
2. Type keywords like "Invoice," "Report," or "Resume" in the search bar.
3. Choose a professional-looking template.
4. Fill in your content without changing the structure.

Business Use Cases for Templates:

- Meeting agendas
- Employee handbooks
- Client proposals
- Business plans

Pro Tip: Customize a template and save it as your company's standard template for consistency.

5. Mail Merge

MAIL MERGE IS A FEATURE that lets you send personalized letters or emails to a list of recipients using a single template.

How to perform Mail Merge:

1. Go to Mailings > Start Mail Merge > Letters.

2. Click Select Recipients > Use Existing List.
3. Insert merge fields (like «First Name», «Company»).
4. Click Finish & Merge > Print Documents or Send Email Messages.

Example Use Case: Sending salary slips to employees, invitation letters for a seminar, or customer appreciation notes.

---

6. Formatting Techniques for Professional Documents

GOOD FORMATTING IMPROVES readability and creates a strong impression. Word provides advanced formatting tools:

Key Formatting Tools:

- **Styles**: Apply consistent formatting to headings and paragraphs.
- **Line Spacing**: Adjust from single to double for readability.
- **Page Layout**: Margins, orientation (portrait/landscape), and page breaks.
- **Header and Footer**: Add page numbers, date, and logo.

Example Tips:

- Use Ctrl + E to center text.
- Use Ctrl + Shift + N to return to normal style.
- Always justify the paragraph for clean alignment.

---

7. Collaborative Features

BUSINESSES OFTEN WORK in teams. Word allows real-time collaboration:

- Use Share to invite team members to edit.
- Use Review > Track Changes to monitor edits.
- Use Comments to leave suggestions without altering the content.

---

8. Exporting and Sharing Documents

MICROSOFT WORD ALLOWS exporting documents in various formats:

- File > Save As > PDF for professional sharing.
- File > Export > Create PDF/XPS Document.

Also, Word supports integration with email clients, allowing documents to be directly attached and sent.

---

9. Keyboard Shortcuts for Efficiency

COMMON SHORTCUTS:

- Ctrl + B = Bold
- Ctrl + U = Underline
- Ctrl + P = Print
- Ctrl + Z = Undo

- Alt + Shift + D = Insert current date

Use shortcuts to save time, especially when editing large documents.

Conclusion

MICROSOFT WORD REMAINS an indispensable tool for business documentation. Whether you're drafting formal letters, detailed reports, or sending hundreds of personalized emails, its wide array of features helps present information clearly and professionally. Mastering Word empowers business professionals to communicate effectively and operate more efficiently.

Chapter 3: Microsoft Outlook and Business Email Etiquette

IN TODAY'S DIGITAL business landscape, email remains the most widely used form of professional communication. Microsoft Outlook, a part of the Microsoft Office suite, is a powerful tool that helps users manage emails, calendars, contacts, tasks, and meetings—all in one place. In this chapter, we'll explore the key features of Outlook, how to use it effectively for business, and how to follow proper email etiquette to maintain professionalism in every interaction.

1. Introduction to Microsoft Outlook

OUTLOOK IS NOT JUST an email client—it is a comprehensive personal information manager. It streamlines business communication, improves productivity, and helps professionals stay organized.

Key Features of Outlook:

- Email management
- Calendar and scheduling
- Task tracking
- Contacts management
- Meeting coordination

Why Outlook is preferred in businesses:

- Integration with Microsoft 365 apps

- Real-time notifications and reminders
- Enterprise-grade security and spam filters
- Mobile accessibility

---

2. Writing Professional Emails

A WELL-CRAFTED EMAIL reflects professionalism, clarity, and respect. Here's a basic structure:

Structure of a Professional Email:

1. **Subject Line** – Clear and concise (e.g., "Meeting Agenda for May 25")
2. **Salutation** – "Dear Mr. Sharma," or "Hi Riya," depending on the formality
3. **Opening Line** – Purpose of the email (e.g., "I am writing to confirm...")
4. **Main Body** – Provide context and relevant details
5. **Closing Line** – Call to action or conclusion (e.g., "Looking forward to your response.")
6. **Sign-Off** – "Regards," "Sincerely," or "Best," followed by your name

Example Email:

Subject: Confirmation of Meeting – Marketing Strategy

Dear Ms. Roy,

I hope you are doing well. This is to confirm our meeting scheduled for Thursday, May 27, at 3:00 PM to discuss the Q3 marketing strategy. The agenda and presentation will be shared by Wednesday.

Please let me know if there are any changes.

Best,

Mrigendra Bharti

Founder, Inkwhirl

---

3. Email Etiquette in Business

PROPER EMAIL ETIQUETTE helps maintain professionalism and avoid misunderstandings.

Top Email Etiquette Tips:

- Use a professional email address (e.g., firstname.lastname@company.com)
- Avoid using slang or emojis
- Use CC and BCC appropriately
- Respond promptly (ideally within 24 hours)
- Avoid writing in ALL CAPS (it appears aggressive)
- Use a clear and relevant subject line
- Attach documents before writing "please find attached"

Pro Tip: Always proofread your email before sending it to avoid grammatical errors and typos.

---

4. Calendar Management

OUTLOOK'S CALENDAR helps in planning and scheduling.

Features of Outlook Calendar:

- Schedule one-time or recurring events
- Set reminders and notifications
- Share calendars with team members
- Sync with mobile devices

How to Create a Meeting Event:

1. Go to Calendar > New Event
2. Add title (e.g., "Monthly Review Meeting")
3. Set date, time, and location
4. Invite attendees
5. Add agenda in the description box
6. Click "Send"

Use Case Example: You schedule a review meeting for your marketing team every second Monday at 11 AM. You can make this a recurring calendar event and Outlook will automatically remind attendees.

5. Task Management in Outlook

TASKS HELP USERS MANAGE to-do lists and track progress.

How to Use Tasks in Outlook:

1. Click on Tasks from the navigation pane
2. Click New Task
3. Add Title (e.g., "Prepare Sales Report")
4. Set due date and priority
5. Add reminders if needed

Best Practices:

- Break down large tasks into sub-tasks
- Use color categories for easy identification
- Set deadlines and reminders for better time management

Example: Task: "Send Invoice to Client X" Due Date: 25 May 2025 Priority: High Reminder: 10 AM on the same day

6. Scheduling and Managing Meetings

OUTLOOK ALLOWS YOU to schedule, accept, and track meetings efficiently.

How to Schedule a Meeting:

1. Go to Calendar > New Meeting
2. Add meeting title, attendees, and location
3. Include the agenda in the message body
4. Choose time and recurrence
5. Send invitation

Features:

- Track RSVPs
- Propose new times
- Join Teams/Zoom meetings directly if integrated

Meeting Etiquette:

- Be on time
- Send agenda in advance
- Mute when not speaking

- Follow up with minutes after the meeting

---

7. Organizing Your Inbox

KEEPING A CLEAN INBOX saves time and improves focus.

Tips to Organize Inbox:

- Use Folders to categorize emails (e.g., Clients, HR, Projects)
- Set Rules to auto-sort incoming emails
- Use Focused Inbox to prioritize important messages
- Archive old conversations to reduce clutter

Pro Tip: Use Flag to mark emails that need follow-up.

---

8. Useful Shortcuts in Outlook

SPEED UP NAVIGATION with these shortcuts:

- Ctrl + R – Reply
- Ctrl + F – Forward
- Ctrl + N – New Email
- Ctrl + Shift + M – Create a message
- Ctrl + 1 – Go to Mail
- Ctrl + 2 – Go to Calendar
- Ctrl + Shift + A – New appointment

Conclusion

MICROSOFT OUTLOOK IS an indispensable tool for business communication. Its features extend far beyond email—enabling efficient scheduling, task tracking, and team collaboration. When combined with strong email etiquette, Outlook not only helps manage daily business operations but also enhances professional reputation and interpersonal relationships. Mastering Outlook means mastering the language and logistics of the modern business world.

Chapter 4: Digital Accounting Tools

IN THE EVOLVING LANDSCAPE of modern business, digital accounting tools have revolutionized how financial data is recorded, analyzed, and reported. Gone are the days of manually recording transactions in bulky ledger books. Today, small businesses, startups, and large enterprises alike rely on software solutions like Tally, Zoho Books, and QuickBooks to manage their accounts with precision, speed, and ease. In this chapter, we will explore these tools, understand their features, and learn how to use them for basic entries and generating financial reports.

---

1. What Are Digital Accounting Tools?

DIGITAL ACCOUNTING tools are software applications designed to manage and record a company's financial transactions. They automate repetitive accounting tasks such as bookkeeping, invoicing, payroll, and report generation.

Benefits of Digital Accounting Tools:

- Reduce manual errors
- Save time and increase efficiency
- Provide real-time financial insights
- Improve compliance and audit readiness
- Enhance collaboration with teams and accountants

---

2. Introduction to Tally

TALLY IS ONE OF THE most popular accounting software used in India. It is user-friendly, GST-compliant, and suitable for businesses of all sizes.

Key Features of Tally:

- Ledger and group creation
- GST-compliant invoicing
- Inventory management
- Payroll and salary calculations
- Financial reporting

Basic Entry Example in Tally: Let's say you receive Rs. 50,000 from a customer for services rendered.

Steps:

1. Go to Accounting Vouchers
2. Select Receipt Voucher (F6)
3. Debit: Cash/Bank Account
4. Credit: Customer's Account
5. Enter amount: Rs. 50,000
6. Save the voucher

Reporting in Tally: Tally provides balance sheets, profit & loss statements, GST reports, and more under the "Display" > "Statements of Accounts."

3. Introduction to Zoho Books

ZOHO BOOKS IS A CLOUD-based accounting software developed by Zoho Corporation. It is ideal for freelancers, small businesses, and service providers.

Key Features of Zoho Books:

- Cloud access from anywhere
- Automated bank feeds
- Project billing and time tracking
- GST and tax filing
- Client portal for real-time collaboration

Basic Entry Example in Zoho Books: Let's say you want to record an expense for office rent of Rs. 20,000.

Steps:

1. Go to Expenses
2. Click + New
3. Select Vendor (e.g., "Office Landlord")
4. Enter Amount: Rs. 20,000
5. Choose Expense Account: "Rent"
6. Click Save

Reporting in Zoho Books: Go to the Reports section to view Profit & Loss, Balance Sheet, Tax Summary, and Receivables/Payables reports.

4. Introduction to QuickBooks

QUICKBOOKS IS A GLOBAL leader in accounting software, developed by Intuit. It's widely used for its clean interface, automation capabilities, and scalable tools for small to medium businesses.

Key Features of QuickBooks:

- Automatic bank reconciliation
- Invoicing and billing
- Budget planning
- Inventory tracking
- Real-time dashboard

Basic Entry Example in QuickBooks: Suppose you sell products worth Rs. 75,000 to a customer.

Steps:

1. Go to Sales > Invoices
2. Click Create Invoice
3. Select customer, enter items sold, and amount: Rs. 75,000
4. Add tax (if applicable)
5. Save and send invoice

Reporting in QuickBooks: The Reports tab includes various standard and customizable reports like Sales by Product/Service, Income Statements, and Cash Flow reports.

5. Comparing Tally, Zoho Books, and QuickBooks

Feature	Tally	Zoho Books	QuickBooks
Platform	Desktop	Cloud	Cloud/ Desktop
GST Ready	Yes	Yes	Yes
Ease of Use	Medium	High	High
Inventory Tracking	Yes	Yes	Yes
Best For	Indian businesses	Startups/ Freelancers	Global SMEs

6. Real-World Use Case

LET'S SAY MRIGENDRA Bharti runs a digital publishing startup. He uses:

- **Tally** for GST filing and local accounting
- **Zoho Books** to manage online subscriptions and automate billing
- **QuickBooks** to collaborate with international clients and accountants

This hybrid use of tools allows his business to operate efficiently across markets and meet regulatory compliance both locally and globally.

7. Best Practices for Using Digital Accounting Tools

- Reconcile bank accounts monthly
- Use automation for recurring entries
- Backup data regularly (for offline tools)

- Restrict user roles and permissions
- Customize templates and invoices to suit branding

Conclusion

DIGITAL ACCOUNTING tools are indispensable in today's business environment. Mastering tools like Tally, Zoho Books, and QuickBooks allows entrepreneurs and finance professionals to manage accounts accurately and focus on strategic growth. Whether you're a startup owner, freelancer, or finance student, gaining hands-on experience in these tools will prepare you for the digital-first future of business accounting.

Chapter 5: Data Visualization Tools

IN THE DIGITAL AGE, data is a powerful resource—but without clear visualization, data can be difficult to interpret or use effectively. This is where data visualization tools come in. They transform raw numbers into interactive charts, graphs, and dashboards that offer insights at a glance. For businesses, effective visualization means faster decision-making, clearer communication, and enhanced strategic planning. In this chapter, we explore three powerful tools: **Power BI**, **Tableau**, and **Google Data Studio**.

---

1. What is Data Visualization?

DATA VISUALIZATION is the graphical representation of information and data. By using visual elements like charts, graphs, and maps, it helps users understand trends, outliers, and patterns in data.

Why Visualization Matters in Business:

- Converts complex data into actionable insights
- Supports data-driven decision-making
- Increases efficiency in reporting
- Makes presentations more engaging and understandable

---

2. Microsoft Power BI

POWER BI is a business analytics tool developed by Microsoft that enables users to visualize data and share insights across an organization. It integrates well with Excel and other Microsoft services.

Key Features:

- Interactive dashboards
- Real-time data updates
- Integration with Excel, Azure, and SQL Server
- Natural language query support (Q&A)

Use Case Example: Imagine a sales team tracking quarterly sales performance across regions.

Steps:

1. Import Excel sales data into Power BI
2. Create a bar chart showing sales per region
3. Add filters for quarter and product category
4. Share dashboard with management via Power BI Service

Business Impact: Quick visualization of underperforming regions helps in re-strategizing marketing efforts.

---

3. Tableau

TABLEAU is a leading data visualization software used globally for business intelligence. It's known for its powerful features and ease of use, even for users with no coding background.

Key Features:

- Drag-and-drop interface
- Advanced analytics using calculated fields
- Data blending and forecasting

- Easy integration with databases (MySQL, Oracle, etc.)

Use Case Example: A retail manager wants to analyze customer footfall and sales volume.

Steps:

1. Connect Tableau to the POS system database
2. Use line charts to visualize hourly footfall
3. Add a map view to show top-performing store locations
4. Highlight trends with color-coded indicators

Business Impact: Enables optimization of staffing schedules and inventory management.

---

4. Google Data Studio

GOOGLE DATA STUDIO is a free tool by Google that turns your data into informative, customizable dashboards and reports. It's ideal for marketing analytics and integrates well with Google products like Google Ads and Analytics.

Key Features:

- Free to use
- Seamless integration with Google services
- Real-time collaboration
- Interactive filters and date ranges

Use Case Example: A digital marketing agency monitors performance across multiple ad campaigns.

Steps:

1. Connect to Google Analytics and Ads
2. Create a dashboard with impressions, CTR, conversions
3. Use filters for campaign, region, and device type
4. Share live report links with clients

Business Impact: Clients get clear visibility into campaign ROI and can make faster decisions on budget allocations.

5. Comparison of the Tools

Feature	Power BI	Tableau	Google Data Studio
Pricing	Freemium/Paid	Paid	Free
Integration	Strong with Microsoft	Broad DB connectivity	Strong with Google stack
Ease of Use	Moderate	Easy	Very Easy
Ideal For	Enterprises, Analysts	SMEs, Data Scientists	Marketers, Freelancers

6. Real-Life Business Scenario

SUPPOSE MRIGENDRA BHARTI'S startup tracks website visits, book sales, and customer support tickets.

- **Power BI** is used internally for financial and HR data analysis.
- **Tableau** is used by the analytics team for product performance.
- **Google Data Studio** provides live dashboards to stakeholders and partners on campaign success.

This multi-tool approach ensures deep internal insights and transparent external reporting.

---

7. Best Practices for Data Visualization

- Choose the right chart for the data (e.g., pie for parts, bar for comparisons)
- Avoid clutter and overuse of colors
- Label charts clearly
- Use filters to allow user-driven exploration
- Ensure data accuracy before presentation

Conclusion

DATA VISUALIZATION tools empower businesses to make sense of their data and communicate findings effectively. Whether it's Power BI's deep analytics, Tableau's flexibility, or Google Data Studio's simplicity, each tool brings unique strengths. Mastering these platforms gives professionals a competitive edge in today's data-driven marketplace.

Chapter 6: Cloud Computing in Business

IN TODAY'S TECHNOLOGY-driven world, businesses demand flexibility, scalability, and efficiency. Cloud computing has emerged as a game-changer, offering a modern solution to traditional IT infrastructure limitations. Whether it's storing files, managing communications, or running software applications, cloud computing makes it all possible with minimal upfront investment. This chapter delves into the concepts of cloud computing and explores popular business tools like Google Workspace, Microsoft 365, and various cloud storage platforms.

1. What is Cloud Computing?

CLOUD COMPUTING IS the delivery of computing services—servers, storage, databases, networking, software, analytics, and intelligence—over the internet ("the cloud") to offer faster innovation, flexible resources, and economies of scale.

Key Characteristics:

- On-demand self-service
- Broad network access
- Resource pooling
- Rapid elasticity
- Measured service

Benefits for Businesses:

- Reduced IT costs
- Remote access and collaboration
- Automatic updates and maintenance
- Enhanced security and disaster recovery

---

2. Types of Cloud Services

CLOUD SERVICES ARE typically classified into three models:

1. IaaS (Infrastructure as a Service): Provides virtualized computing resources over the internet. Example: Amazon Web Services (AWS).

2. PaaS (Platform as a Service): Offers hardware and software tools over the internet, mainly for application development. Example: Google App Engine.

3. SaaS (Software as a Service): Delivers software applications over the internet, accessible via a browser without installation. Example: Microsoft 365, Google Workspace.

---

3. Google Workspace

GOOGLE WORKSPACE (formerly G Suite) is a suite of cloud-based productivity and collaboration tools developed by Google.

Includes:

- Gmail (professional email service)
- Google Docs, Sheets, Slides (document creation)
- Google Drive (cloud storage)

- Google Meet & Chat (video conferencing & messaging)
- Google Calendar (schedule and manage meetings)

Business Example: A remote marketing team collaborates in real-time using Google Docs to draft proposals and conducts daily meetings over Google Meet. Google Drive ensures all project files are accessible 24/7, improving workflow and reducing delays.

---

4. Microsoft 365

MICROSOFT 365 is a subscription-based cloud service that includes familiar Office applications and other productivity services.

Includes:

- Microsoft Word, Excel, PowerPoint (document management)
- Outlook (email)
- OneDrive (cloud storage)
- Teams (team communication and meetings)
- SharePoint (internal team site)

Business Example: A legal firm stores all case documents in OneDrive, edits them using Word Online, and schedules weekly client meetings through Microsoft Teams. This setup enables secure, centralized, and collaborative document management.

---

5. Cloud Storage Tools

CLOUD STORAGE ALLOWS businesses to store data on the internet through a cloud computing provider who manages and operates data storage as a service.

Popular Tools:

- **Google Drive:** 15 GB free, seamless integration with Google Workspace.
- **Dropbox:** Known for its simplicity and fast sync.
- **OneDrive:** Integrated with Microsoft services, ideal for Microsoft 365 users.
- **iCloud:** Common among Apple users, good for syncing between iOS/macOS devices.

Features:

- File sharing and permission settings
- Auto-sync across devices
- Data backup and version history

Use Case: An event management company saves all contracts, designs, and schedules on Dropbox. Team members can access or update files on their phones during on-site events.

---

6. Advantages of Cloud Computing in Business

- **Cost-Effective:** No upfront hardware costs, pay-as-you-go model.

- **Scalable:** Businesses can scale up or down based on demand.
- **Reliable:** Multiple backups and disaster recovery options.
- **Accessible:** Work from anywhere with internet access.
- **Secure:** Encryption, authentication, and regular audits by cloud providers.

---

7. Challenges and Considerations

WHILE CLOUD COMPUTING offers numerous benefits, businesses must also be mindful of certain limitations:

- **Data Security & Privacy:** Ensuring compliance with regulations (like GDPR).
- **Internet Dependency:** Downtime can affect access.
- **Vendor Lock-in:** Difficulty in migrating between services.
- **Cost Management:** Unmonitored usage may lead to unexpected charges.

Tip: Use cost-monitoring tools and conduct regular data audits to manage expenses and maintain data integrity.

---

8. Real-Life Application Scenario

A GROWING E-COMMERCE startup uses:

- Google Workspace for internal collaboration
- Microsoft 365 for detailed data reporting via Excel

- Dropbox for backup of all design and media files

This hybrid cloud approach ensures efficient operations, secure data handling, and real-time team collaboration across geographies.

9. Best Practices for Using Cloud Tools

- Use strong passwords and enable two-factor authentication
- Backup important files regularly
- Train employees on cloud security awareness
- Limit user access based on roles
- Monitor storage usage and optimize regularly

Conclusion

CLOUD COMPUTING IS no longer an option—it's a necessity for modern businesses. Whether it's through SaaS tools like Google Workspace and Microsoft 365, or through robust cloud storage options, businesses that embrace the cloud enjoy a competitive advantage. Understanding the core concepts and tools helps professionals make informed decisions and drive digital transformation with confidence.

Chapter 7: E-Commerce Applications

THE DIGITAL ECONOMY has seen explosive growth in recent years, and at the heart of this transformation lies e-commerce. Businesses, small and large, have adopted e-commerce platforms to reach customers globally, reduce operational costs, and increase revenue. This chapter explores how popular platforms like Amazon, Flipkart, and Shopify work, and explains business models like B2B, B2C, and the concept of dropshipping.

---

1. What is E-Commerce?

E-COMMERCE (ELECTRONIC commerce) refers to the buying and selling of goods or services using the internet, and the transfer of money and data to execute these transactions.

Categories of E-Commerce:

- **B2B (Business to Business):** Transactions between businesses (e.g., Alibaba)
- **B2C (Business to Consumer):** Direct sale from business to end-user (e.g., Amazon)
- **C2C (Consumer to Consumer):** Individuals selling to individuals (e.g., eBay)
- **C2B (Consumer to Business):** Individuals offer products/ services to companies (e.g., freelancing platforms)

---

2. Working of Amazon

AMAZON is one of the world's largest e-commerce platforms, known for its vast product range, customer-centric policies, and efficient logistics.

How It Works:

- Sellers register and list their products.
- Customers browse and place orders.
- Amazon handles order processing, payments, and delivery (via Fulfillment by Amazon - FBA).
- Customer support and return logistics are integrated.

Example: A small electronics business lists products on Amazon. Through FBA, Amazon stores, packs, and ships items, allowing the seller to focus on inventory and growth.

---

3. Working of Flipkart

FLIPKART is a major Indian e-commerce player with similar operational mechanisms to Amazon but with unique regional strategies.

Key Features:

- Cash on Delivery (popular in India)
- Local language support
- Flipkart Assured (quality and delivery assurance)

Business Model:

- Hybrid model of marketplace and direct sales.

Example: A seller lists ethnic wear on Flipkart. Flipkart's promotional tools help them reach a broader audience during festive seasons, boosting sales.

---

4. Shopify – Create Your Own Store

SHOPIFY is a cloud-based platform that allows individuals and businesses to create their own online stores without needing to code.

Features:

- Website templates and themes
- Payment gateway integration
- Inventory and shipping management
- App store for additional functionality

Use Case: An artist launches a Shopify store to sell digital art and prints. With built-in SEO and marketing tools, they drive traffic via social media.

---

5. Dropshipping Model

DROPSHIPPING IS A RETAIL fulfillment method where a store doesn't keep the products it sells in stock. Instead, it purchases the item from a third-party supplier and has it shipped directly to the customer.

Advantages:

- Low startup costs
- No inventory management

- Wide product selection

Disadvantages:

- Lower profit margins
- Limited control over shipping and quality
- High competition

Example: An entrepreneur sets up a Shopify store, integrates it with a dropshipping supplier, and markets niche products via Instagram. Orders are fulfilled by the supplier directly.

---

6. B2B vs. B2C Models

Feature	B2B	B2C
Target Audience	Businesses	Individual consumers
Purchase Volume	Large, bulk purchases	Single, small transactions
Pricing	Negotiable, volume-based	Fixed, listed prices
Decision Making	Rational, value-driven	Emotional, needs-based
Relationship	Long-term partnerships	Short-term interactions

EXAMPLE OF B2B: A restaurant orders kitchen equipment in bulk from a commercial supplier's e-commerce portal.

Example of B2C: A student orders a laptop from Amazon for personal use.

---

7. Real-life Case Study

A FASHION ENTREPRENEUR uses Shopify to set up a branded store, integrates print-on-demand services, and uses Instagram marketing to drive traffic. Over time, she expands by listing on Amazon for additional visibility, managing both B2C sales and B2B partnerships with local retailers.

---

8. Emerging Trends in E-Commerce

- **Voice Commerce:** Shopping via voice assistants like Alexa.
- **AR/VR Shopping:** Virtual try-ons for clothes and furniture.
- **AI in E-Commerce:** Chatbots, product recommendations, inventory forecasting.
- **Social Commerce:** Shopping directly through platforms like Instagram and Facebook.

---

9. Tips for Success in E-Commerce

- Use high-quality product images and descriptions.
- Offer multiple payment options.
- Provide excellent customer service.
- Analyze customer data and feedback.
- Invest in SEO and digital marketing.

Conclusion

E-COMMERCE IS RESHAPING the global economy. Understanding its applications—whether through giants like Amazon and Flipkart, or by launching personal stores on Shopify—gives aspiring entrepreneurs and business professionals the power to tap into new markets and customers. With low entry barriers and endless possibilities, the digital marketplace continues to grow rapidly.

Chapter 8: Cybersecurity and Data Protection

IN TODAY'S INCREASINGLY digital business world, cybersecurity is not just a technical issue—it's a business imperative. Cyber threats are becoming more sophisticated, and companies, regardless of size, are potential targets. This chapter discusses essential aspects of cybersecurity, including password hygiene, phishing, malware threats, and practical data protection techniques used in business environments.

---

1. Introduction to Cybersecurity

CYBERSECURITY REFERS to the practice of protecting systems, networks, and programs from digital attacks. These attacks are often aimed at accessing, changing, or destroying sensitive information, interrupting normal business processes, or extorting money from users.

Why It Matters:

- Prevent financial losses
- Protect brand reputation
- Ensure legal and regulatory compliance

---

2. Password Hygiene

PASSWORD HYGIENE refers to the best practices for creating and maintaining strong passwords.

Best Practices:

- Use long and complex passwords (at least 12 characters)
- Avoid using personal information (name, birthdate)
- Never reuse passwords across multiple accounts
- Use password managers like LastPass, Bitwarden, or 1Password
- Enable two-factor authentication (2FA) wherever possible

Example: Instead of using "company123", use a passphrase like "My$Biz@2025IsSafe!" and store it securely in a password manager.

3. Understanding Phishing Attacks

PHISHING IS A CYBERATTACK where attackers disguise themselves as legitimate entities to trick people into providing sensitive data like login credentials or credit card numbers.

Types of Phishing:

- **Email Phishing:** Fake emails with malicious links
- **Spear Phishing:** Targeted attack using personal information
- **Smishing:** SMS-based phishing
- **Vishing:** Voice call scams

Signs of Phishing:

- Urgent language ("Your account will be locked!")
- Suspicious links or email addresses

- Unexpected attachments

Example: An employee receives an email that looks like it's from their bank asking to verify account details. Instead of clicking the link, they verify the email's origin with IT support.

---

4. Malware and Its Impact

MALWARE is malicious software designed to damage, disrupt, or gain unauthorized access to a system.

Types of Malware:

- **Virus:** Attaches to files and spreads
- **Worms:** Self-replicating and spread across networks
- **Trojan Horse:** Disguised as legitimate software
- **Ransomware:** Locks data and demands payment
- **Spyware:** Secretly gathers user data

Example: A business downloads a seemingly harmless PDF invoice from an unknown vendor. It's a Trojan, which installs ransomware and locks down company files.

Prevention:

- Use updated antivirus software
- Avoid downloading attachments from unknown sources
- Regularly update systems and software

---

5. Business Data Protection Techniques

PROTECTING SENSITIVE business data is crucial for operational continuity and compliance.

Effective Methods:

1. **Data Encryption:** Protects data in transit and at rest.
2. **Access Control:** Limit data access to authorized personnel only.
3. **Regular Backups:** Store backups off-site or in the cloud.
4. **Network Firewalls:** Prevent unauthorized access.
5. **Security Policies:** Train employees on secure practices.
6. **Monitoring & Auditing:** Log activities for compliance and anomaly detection.

Example: A company implements role-based access control. Only HR personnel can access employee salary data, reducing internal data breach risks.

---

6. Cybersecurity in Remote Work

WITH THE RISE OF HYBRID and remote work models, new risks have emerged.

Secure Remote Practices:

- Use Virtual Private Networks (VPNs)
- Avoid public Wi-Fi or use secured hotspots
- Encrypt emails and use secure cloud services
- Regular device audits and antivirus updates

Example: An employee working from home accesses sensitive data using a VPN and saves files to a secure, encrypted Google Workspace account.

---

7. Legal and Compliance Aspects

DATA PROTECTION LAWS require businesses to secure customer and employee information.

Key Regulations:

- **GDPR (Europe):** Protects personal data of EU citizens
- **HIPAA (USA):** Health data protection
- **IT Act (India):** Includes provisions for data protection and cybercrime

Example: An e-commerce business operating in the EU must ensure compliance with GDPR or face heavy penalties for data breaches.

---

8. Real-world Case Study

TARGET CORPORATION (2013 breach): Hackers used credentials stolen from a third-party HVAC vendor to access Target's payment systems, compromising over 40 million credit and debit card records.

Lesson: Cybersecurity is not just about internal systems—it includes vendor management.

---

9. Tips to Build a Cyber-Secure Culture

- Conduct regular training sessions for employees
- Send simulated phishing tests
- Establish a cybersecurity response team

- Audit systems frequently
- Encourage reporting of suspicious activity

---

10. Conclusion

CYBERSECURITY IS A shared responsibility. It is vital for every business to adopt a proactive, layered approach to defend against cyber threats. Simple practices like password hygiene and recognizing phishing emails, combined with robust data protection tools, can significantly reduce business risk.

Chapter 9: Digital Marketing Tools and Analytics

DIGITAL MARKETING HAS revolutionized the way businesses reach and engage with their target audiences. With the rise of online platforms, companies now have access to powerful tools and analytics to optimize marketing efforts, increase visibility, and drive conversions. This chapter explores key components of digital marketing including SEO, SEM, Google Ads, Meta (Facebook & Instagram) Ads, analytics dashboards, and email marketing tools.

---

1. Introduction to Digital Marketing

DIGITAL MARKETING ENCOMPASSES all marketing efforts that use electronic devices or the internet. Businesses leverage digital channels such as search engines, social media, email, and websites to connect with current and prospective customers.

Key Benefits:

- Cost-effective
- Measurable and data-driven
- Enables targeted marketing
- Real-time performance monitoring

---

2. Search Engine Optimization (SEO)

SEO INVOLVES OPTIMIZING websites to rank higher in search engine results pages (SERPs) organically.

Components of SEO:

- **On-Page SEO:** Content quality, keyword usage, meta tags, image optimization
- **Off-Page SEO:** Backlinks from trusted sources
- **Technical SEO:** Site speed, mobile-friendliness, secure connection (HTTPS)

Example: A travel blog writing articles with keywords like "best places to visit in 2025" will likely appear higher in Google search when those keywords are used.

Tools:

- Google Search Console
- SEMrush
- Ahrefs

---

3. Search Engine Marketing (SEM)

UNLIKE SEO, SEM INVOLVES paid strategies to improve visibility on search engines.

Popular Platforms:

- Google Ads
- Bing Ads

SEM Strategies:

- Keyword targeting

- Ad copy optimization
- Bidding and budgeting
- A/B testing of ads

Example: An online clothing store runs Google Ads targeting the keyword "buy cotton shirts online." The ad appears on top of Google's results, leading to more clicks and potential sales.

---

4. Google Ads

GOOGLE ADS ALLOWS BUSINESSES to create search, display, video, and shopping ads on Google's advertising network.

Types of Google Ads:

- **Search Ads:** Appear on SERPs
- **Display Ads:** Visual banners on websites
- **Shopping Ads:** Product listings
- **Video Ads:** YouTube advertisements

Metrics to Monitor:

- Click-Through Rate (CTR)
- Cost Per Click (CPC)
- Conversion Rate

Example: A digital marketing agency uses Google Ads to promote their webinar and sets a budget of ₹500/day to drive registrations.

---

5. Meta Ads (Facebook & Instagram)

META ADS MANAGER HELPS run ads on Facebook, Instagram, and Messenger.

Targeting Features:

- Custom Audiences (based on customer data)
- Lookalike Audiences (similar to existing customers)
- Detailed demographics and interests

Ad Types:

- Image & Video ads
- Carousel ads
- Stories ads
- Collection ads

Example: A food delivery startup runs Instagram Story ads targeting users aged 18–30 in Mumbai with a 30% discount offer.

---

6. Analytics Dashboards

ANALYTICS DASHBOARDS provide real-time insights into digital performance, helping businesses make data-driven decisions.

Popular Tools:

- **Google Analytics:** Tracks website traffic, user behavior, and conversions

- **Google Looker Studio (formerly Data Studio):** Visual reporting
- **Meta Insights:** Performance of Facebook and Instagram campaigns
- **Hotjar:** User session recordings and heatmaps

Example: An e-commerce business uses Google Analytics to track which product pages are most visited and where users drop off during checkout.

---

7. Email Marketing Tools

EMAIL MARKETING REMAINS a powerful channel for customer retention and engagement.

Popular Tools:

- Mailchimp
- ConvertKit
- Constant Contact
- Sendinblue

Common Use Cases:

- Welcome emails
- Newsletters
- Cart abandonment reminders
- Promotional campaigns

Example: An online course platform sends a weekly newsletter to subscribers with new blog posts, course updates, and offers using Mailchimp.

Best Practices:

- Personalize emails
- Segment audiences
- Use clear CTAs (Call to Actions)
- Optimize for mobile

---

8. Integrating Marketing Tools

MODERN BUSINESSES OFTEN integrate various tools for a seamless marketing workflow.

Example Stack:

- **Google Ads + Google Analytics:** Track ad ROI
- **Facebook Ads + CRM tools (e.g., HubSpot):** Lead tracking
- **Email marketing + e-commerce platform:** Automated product suggestions based on purchase history

---

9. Case Study: A Small Business Success

BUSINESS: A local bakery **Strategy:**

- Used Instagram and Facebook ads for local promotions

- Optimized Google My Business for SEO
- Sent weekly newsletters with new menu items
- Used Google Analytics to see what time users visit the site

Outcome:

- Increased walk-ins by 40%
- Online orders grew by 60% in three months

---

10. Conclusion

DIGITAL MARKETING TOOLS and analytics empower businesses to operate smarter, not harder. Whether you are optimizing for search engines, running paid ads, or engaging customers via email, a well-executed digital strategy backed by accurate data can lead to substantial business growth.

Chapter 10: Business Communication through IT

EFFECTIVE COMMUNICATION is the backbone of any successful business. In the digital age, communication tools have evolved far beyond traditional emails and phone calls. Today's businesses use platforms like Slack, Zoom, and Microsoft Teams to facilitate real-time communication, collaboration, and productivity. This chapter explores the use of these tools and their significance in modern business communication.

1. Introduction to Business Communication through IT

BUSINESS COMMUNICATION through IT refers to the use of digital tools and platforms to exchange information, share ideas, conduct meetings, and collaborate on projects in a business environment.

Key Benefits:

- Enhances team collaboration
- Speeds up decision-making
- Supports remote work culture
- Maintains a record of communication

Example: A remote software development team uses Microsoft Teams to discuss project updates, share files, and host daily stand-up meetings.

2. Business Chats and Instant Messaging

INSTANT MESSAGING TOOLS are widely used for quick, informal, and efficient communication among team members.

Popular Platforms:

- Slack
- Microsoft Teams
- Google Chat
- Skype for Business

Features:

- One-on-one and group chats
- File sharing
- Emojis and reactions for quick feedback
- Integration with other apps (e.g., Trello, Asana)

Example: A marketing team uses Slack channels to brainstorm ideas and instantly notify team members about client feedback.

Best Practices:

- Keep messages clear and concise
- Use threads to maintain context
- Avoid spamming group chats with non-urgent topics

---

3. Video Calls and Virtual Meetings

VIDEO CONFERENCING has become an essential tool for face-to-face interaction in remote and hybrid work models.

Popular Platforms:

- Zoom
- Microsoft Teams
- Google Meet
- Cisco Webex

Uses:

- Daily stand-ups and team meetings
- Client presentations and product demos
- Online interviews and webinars

Example: An HR department uses Zoom to conduct virtual onboarding sessions for new employees across different locations.

Tips for Effective Video Calls:

- Choose a quiet environment
- Dress professionally
- Mute yourself when not speaking
- Share agenda beforehand

---

4. Slack for Business Communication

SLACK IS A WIDELY ADOPTED platform for internal business communication.

Core Features:

- Channels for specific projects or teams
- Direct messages (DMs)
- Integration with apps like Google Drive, GitHub, Jira
- Slackbot for reminders and automated responses

Example: A sales team creates separate Slack channels for leads, negotiations, and customer support, streamlining communication and follow-ups.

Benefits:

- Organized communication
- Real-time updates
- Reduces email clutter

---

5. Microsoft Teams for Collaboration

MICROSOFT TEAMS IS part of the Microsoft 365 suite and offers a comprehensive workspace for teamwork.

Key Features:

- Team-specific channels and chat threads
- Integration with Outlook, Word, Excel, and SharePoint

- Built-in meeting scheduler
- File sharing and co-authoring

Example: A finance team uses Teams to co-edit budget reports while discussing changes on a video call, increasing efficiency and transparency.

6. Zoom for Virtual Communication

ZOOM IS BEST KNOWN for its user-friendly interface and reliability in video conferencing.

Core Features:

- HD video and audio
- Screen sharing and whiteboard
- Breakout rooms
- Webinar hosting

Example: An education startup uses Zoom to conduct virtual classes, workshops, and team meetings with breakout rooms for group discussions.

Security Tip: Always use meeting passwords and enable the waiting room feature to prevent unauthorized access.

7. Productivity Gains through IT Communication

USING IT TOOLS FOR business communication enhances productivity in several ways:

- **Reduced Email Overload:** Teams communicate directly via chat platforms.

- **Faster Decision-Making:** Real-time messaging and video calls speed up discussions.

- **Centralized Information:** Shared files and discussion histories are accessible in one place.

- **Remote Work Support:** Allows seamless operations regardless of physical location.

---

8. Integrating Communication Tools with Business Processes

MODERN IT COMMUNICATION tools integrate with project management, CRM, and file storage platforms.

Example Integrations:

- Slack + Trello: Task updates in Slack
- Teams + OneDrive: Direct file access in chats
- Zoom + Calendars: Automated meeting scheduling

---

9. Case Study: Remote Startup Team

SCENARIO: A remote digital agency with 12 members across India

Tools Used:

- Slack for team chat and updates
- Zoom for client calls
- Teams for project collaboration

Results:

- 30% increase in project turnaround time
- 40% fewer internal emails
- Improved client satisfaction due to better coordination

---

10. Conclusion

BUSINESS COMMUNICATION through IT tools like Slack, Zoom, and Microsoft Teams has transformed the workplace into a more flexible, connected, and productive environment. As businesses grow and adapt to hybrid or remote models, mastering these tools is essential for efficient communication and operational success.

www.ingramcontent.com/pod-product-compliance
Lightning Source LLC
LaVergne TN
LVHW022028200926
848481LV00007B/2585
* 9 7 9 8 2 3 1 6 3 7 5 0 8 *